FROM COUNTRY T[...]

Romford Market Within L[...]

CW01095298

by

Norma Jennings, Nellie Sims
& George Saddington

With the Pupils of Redden Court School

*"Occasionally a body of factual knowledge does
exist only in the memories of men and women
and it would be lost, or greatly attenuated, were
it not taken down before they died."*
George Ewart Evans

Origination by Alan Bauckham
Published by Redden Court Enterprises
and London Borough of Havering Libraries

Reprinted by The Lavenham Press 2002
© Norma Jennings, Nellie Sims and George Saddington 1996
ISBN 0 9528725 0 1

CONTENTS

A Historic Perspective   5

From Country...   9

...To Cockney   15

Ever Been Had?   21

The Wednesday Market Remembered   23

A Market "Who was Who"   31

Memories of the Saturday Market   39

The Perimeter   46

The Market Today   55

ESSEX EDUCATION COMMITTEE.   ATTENDANCE CARD.

THE MARKET PLACE, ROMFORD, ESSEX.

Before the Second World War, cards such as this were presented to Essex school pupils who had achieved one week's full attendance.

ACKNOWLEDGEMENTS

When we decided that we would like to produce a booklet to celebrate the 750th anniversary of Romford market we were fortunate to have on our staff Mr. Bauckham, a desk top publisher and photographer, and Mrs. Jennings, a teacher, local historian and author who grew up in Romford. We were delighted when Mrs. Nellie Sims, a well-known market celebrity and close neighbour of the school, and Mr. Saddington, Chief Librarian of all the libraries in Havering, also accepted our invitation to join us in our venture.

Over 500 pupils interviewed at least two people each in order to gather as much information as possible on the market. We would have needed an encyclopaedia to do full justice to the subject but we could only afford to publish a small booklet. We hope, nevertheless, that we have managed to capture something of the atmosphere of the market over the years in words and pictures and should like to apologize, now, for any omissions. Although we received much detailed information from many, we should like to single out two who have been of particular help to us: Mr. Bob Hollowbread, a friend of Stewart Adams, who ran a stall in the market from 1965 and Mr. Charlie Fancourt, Carly Norris's grandfather, who founded a market dynasty. We should also like to acknowledge the contribution of Mr. Henry Crossley, grandfather of Lisa Crossley, who allowed us to quote from his book "Grandfather's Romford".

In addition to those friends, neighbours and relatives of the pupils who gave us so much help but are too numerous to mention individually, we should like to thank the following for information given or illustrations supplied: Mr. Roy Alexander, Mr. Steve Bowley, Mr. and Mrs. C. Bridgen, Mr. Chapman, Mr. J. Dodds, Essex Record Office, Mrs. K. Fowler and Mrs. J. Hall, both née Hollowell, Havering Libraries: Reference and Information Department, Mr. Barry Jones, Mrs. Cathleen Jones, Mr. Donald Law, Mrs. Beryl Nelson, Mrs. Jean Sherry, Mr. Roy Squire, Mrs. Vera Thomas.

Mrs. Olive Wiles and Mr. Norman Jennings deserve a special mention for all their advice and encouragement, as do our three authors and Mr. Alan Bauckham who have given freely of their own time. Mr. K. Ratley too, allowed us to use his photograph on the front cover free of charge.

We should also like to thank those market traders who gave one of our classes such a warm welcome on what proved to be a very cold day when they were doing research for the booklet, notably: Mr. Brandon Snr., Mr. Childs Snr., Mr. Childs Jnr.(better known as Billy Beet), Mr. and Mrs. H. Crosbie, Mr. Jim Currie, Mr. Charlie Fancourt Jnr., Mr. Eddie Fancourt, Mr. G.Finegold, Mr. Tony Gore, Mr. Tony Luscombe, Mr. Ian Mackay, Mr. Ernie Preedy, Mr. Rider, Mr. George Wyre (better known as Brummy) and Wickenden Meats. The Market Manager, Mr. Harvey Read, helped us enormously and came up to the school to talk about the present day market.

Although this is a booklet of modest size, it was nevertheless beyond the school's resources to finance it alone, and we are indebted to those who sponsored it or made a donation. These firms and individuals are listed inside the booklet's back cover. The financial burden was further alleviated by the offer from Havering Libraries' Service to help us publish it. Proceeds from sale of the booklet will go to the Redden Court pupils' Enterprise Fund, from which a donation will be made to St.Francis Hospice, the present day market traders' favourite charity.

From a painting of Romford market, dated 1880, which hangs in Central Library.

A HISTORIC PERSPECTIVE

For 200 years the town of Romford has been closely identified with its market and brewery. Sadly the Romford brewery is no more but the market has survived to celebrate its 750th anniversary in 1997. This volume deals with a particular period of the market's history; the change from a predominantly rural economy to the one with which we are familiar today. It is also the story of the growing influence of the East End trader within the market and the declining importance of the Essex farmer.

However, there is a need to set this short but important period in the development of our market into the context of the entire 750 years of its fascinating history and it is to be hoped that this thumbnail sketch of the establishment and development of the market will give a flavour of over seven centuries of market trading.

Romford market was founded in 1247 by permission of King Henry III. There is still a commonly held belief that Henry granted Romford a charter for its market, but this is not so. The King was actually the owner of the market lands and therefore all that was required to establish the new venture was for the Sheriff of Essex to announce the fact by public proclamation throughout the county and for Henry's intention to be entered in the Close Rolls. The King, in all probability, would have known the area from his visits to the Royal Palace at Havering-atte-Bower, built by Edward the Confessor and situated only a few miles to the north, but whether Henry was personally interested in the market transaction can only be a matter for speculation. What we do know is that those astute medieval entrepreneurs who sought the King's permission for a market in Romford knew what they were about, for the enterprise was sufficiently robust to survive the Black Death and Bubonic Plague, two major Civil Wars, royal and religious upheavals, major economic change, and, in more recent times, the threats of Hitler's bomb and rocket attacks during World War Two.

Much of the new market's success must be attributed to its excellent location, situated as it was at the strategically important crossing of the road from London to Colchester with the Havering-atte-Bower to Hornchurch road. London was within easy reach, the Thames only a few miles away, local supplies of fresh water were available, and with immediate access to the leather trade of nearby Hornchurch and the agricultural produce of south-west Essex farmlands, the future of the market seemed assured.

The Romford of 1247 had grown from a small settlement dating from at least Roman times to a town of roughly a thousand population living in an area that approximates with the present North Street, South Street, High Street and Market area. The development of the market is also the development of Romford itself, and the market has always been central to the Romford economy attracting traders, customers and visitors from a wide area for the buying and selling of livestock and crops, and of course bringing with it all the normal supporting trades and professions such as lawyers, bankers, publicans, doctors, blacksmiths and auctioneers to name but a few.

The improvements in communications over the centuries strengthened Romford's trading position and the town's economy and size grew. The Thames ferry services linked Essex (and Romford) to the agriculture of Kent; stage and mail coaches travelling to East Anglia and the coast would often stop in the market, some to change or water their horses at the market place inns; and the coming of the steam railway not only linked Romford to Central and East London but also to Chelmsford and other Essex towns.

Market Days

Although Wednesday was stipulated as the original market day, market days have varied over the centuries. During the 18th century Romford market had a fine reputation for grain and was one of the few markets in Essex dealing in corn. Prior to 1800 there are records of regular Monday sales of hogs and Tuesday sales of fattened calves, with Wednesday continuing to be the main market day for a variety of livestock and farm produce. The definition of livestock was extended in an extraordinary way in 1831 with one of the great market stories which concerned a certain Thomas Newcombe who brought his wife, in a halter, to Romford and auctioned her in the market for five shillings and sixpence with a further sixpence added for the new rope purchased by him to tie her to a market post

Many consider the period from the late 19th century to the First World War to be the heyday of the market and for a flavour of what Romford market life must have been like at this time the reader is referred to Charles Hussey's colourful essay " Romford and its Market" (1897). The scene painted by the author is fascinating with his descriptions of the sale of farm livestock as well as "every conceivable domestic animal", together with the doings of the regular market characters of the time including the rope-maker, basket weaver, market entertainer, quack doctor and even the army recruiting sergeant.

Problems Ahead

The tolls and dues of the market belonged to the Lord of the Manor and until 1828 the manor was owned by the Crown. In 1828 the manor, including the market rights, was sold to Hugh McIntosh of Havering. The market remained in private hands for over sixty years, but with increasing acrimony between the owners and the Romford Local Board (the forerunner of today's Borough Council) who were anxious to see improvements to the paving, lighting and hygiene of the market place which, until 1860,was unpaved and described in a report of the day as "waste ground and soil". In 1892 the government's Board of Agriculture ordered that the market should be closed down and the following uncertain days must have been a critically low point in the history of the market, causing widespread consternation among the residents of Romford. However, the Romford Local Board stepped in and bought the market from the McIntosh family, thus enabling them to carry out the necessary improvements and save the market and many livelihoods in the process. Since that time the market has been administered continuously by the Local Authority.

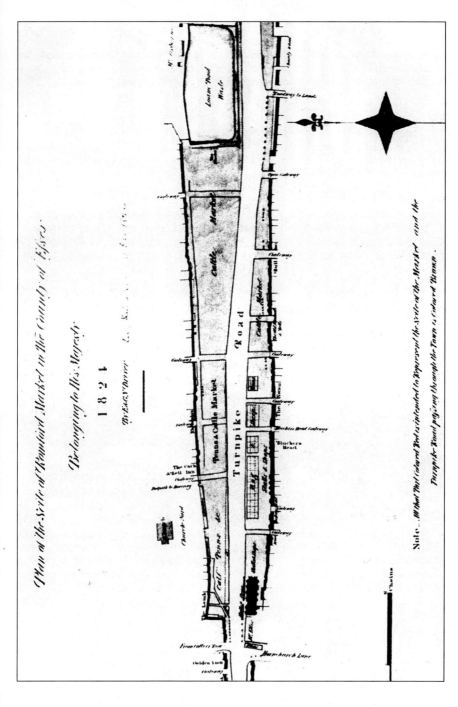

Plan of market dated 1824. Only a small amount of space was occupied by shops and stalls.

7

Pigs and cattle are driven along the High Street (London Road), past the Golden Lion, to and from the market in the closing years of the 19th century. Note the condition of the road.

FROM COUNTRY.......

In 1803, Romford was described as a small country market town centred upon a long market plain. A population, then, of 3,000 people had swelled to 115,600 by 1963, shortly before Romford was absorbed into the London Borough of Havering.

Livestock was driven "on the hoof" to one of Romford's three weekly markets from within a thirty mile radius and sometimes from as far afield as Wales and Scotland. During the town's Midsummer cattle fair, where much of the cattle trader's business was transacted, droves could block the streets for hours at a time. Other produce for sale reflected the farming life: butter and eggs to profit the farmers' wives; baskets and sacks; rabbits and pheasants for the table; and saws, shovels, bushel measures, rakes, mattocks, scythes, pitchforks and a host of other tools of husbandry.

One-hundred years later, at the turn of the century, the tenor of rural life seemed to have changed little: sheep and cattle thronging the roads leading to the market, farmers in their best clothes, the milling crowds, a horse dealer running a frightened horse, cart horses drawing heavy wagons, all mingling with the barking of dogs, the noise of the livestock, the clatter of hooves upon cobbles and the shouting of drovers, heard long before they hove into view. But the invention of the steam engine was steadily having an impact on this centuries-old scene. Steam haulage was replacing horses on the farm while the railways were revolutionizing the transport of both people and animals; new, efficient methods which were killing off the ancient seasonal fairs, previously among the most important venues for the serious buying and selling of livestock, be it horses, geese, sheep or cattle.

Pedlars and all manner of showmen also converged at these livestock fairs to create an event eagerly anticipated by the entire community. It became a rare respite from toil for which they would save up all year. This "fun" aspect of the fair is all that would remain when the farmers' custom was diverted, intead, to the more efficient weekly livestock markets which were expanding apace. And, at the close of the livestock sales in Romford market, when all the animals were gone and the plain had been hosed down, the market still teemed with life late into the evening. The auctioneers' rostra, and pens vacated by the animals, were commandeered by those merchants who for so long had made a living by travelling from fair to fair throughout the country and who, for some fifty years previously, had been infiltrating the markets to protect their livelihood. These exiles dealt in every conceivable commodity: sweets, clothes, toys, linen, crockery and a variety of cheap, mass-produced articles both for home and personal use.

The slow drawl and comfortable, rounded vowels which once characterised the real "owd Essex boy and gal", and which survive still in pockets north of Brentwood, were increasingly drowned by raucous cries which owed more to the rapid, strident speech of the Cockney costermonger.

A fine group of pigs being driven away from Romford market c.1908. Essex had been renowned for its pigs since medieval times but this breed of black pigs tended to produce too much fat.

The north side of the market c.1910, towards its top, eastern end, in the direction of Gidea Park. (Reproduced by courtesy of Essex Record Office)

The Forgotten Sounds of Romford Market
Although on market days in Rumford (as it was pronounced then) the farmer might sport his best riding boots, he favoured for daily use heavy hob-nailed boots which would stand up to to the rigours of work on the land. He, together with the drover and farm labourer, disdained shoes which were disparagingly referred to as "low shews" or "ankle jacks".

A deal was "jonnick" if it was honest and straight up, as was reliable gossip, "and that's jonnick." The "owd" men would be "settin' down" outside one of the market public houses instead of "gooin' to wuk" while the children, predictably, would be "gittin' dutty" in the dust of the market place or playing "cetch" with some scrap of rubbish. A farmer might buy "fower sockling calves" (four suckling calves), a stallholder sell a great number, "a mort", of baskets, and an impatient hustler receive a tart retort from the discerning housewife pondering over a puchase, "Don't you git ring-a-twisty with me yoong man."

A pig was a "hog" but a "hogget" was a year-old sheep. A "four tooth" was a two year-old sheep, a "bud" a year-old calf, a "baconer" a pig sold for bacon and a "cob" a compact, punchy horse. "Broken mouthed" sheep were those fit only for the abattoir; a "master cow", despite its female gender, was the leader of the herd; and the term "mother-in-law" took on an entirely new meaning when applied to a sheep suckling lambs which were not her own.

The last remnant of the old dialect disappeared in more recent years when the Rumford Shopping Hall was repainted and renamed the Romford Shopping Hall.

The End of the Cattle Market
In the early years of the 20th century, the petrol engine was a further agent of change, the lorry eventually ousting the heavy horse from its last stronghold - between the shafts of cart and wagon. And, as surrounding farmland was sold for housing development to accommodate the town's expanding population, so the small rural community was transformed into an urban sprawl. The three weekly livestock markets were concentrated into one, held on Wednesdays, while on Fridays and Saturdays a general commodities market developed to meet the needs of a different breed of resident. By the 1930s Romford was billed as the shopping centre of south-east England. During its declining years in the 1950s, the cattle market was subsidised by the open-air stall market and ended its life in 1958.

Sheep, cattle, horses, carts, wagons and not a motor vehicle in sight, nor a man without a hat. Romford market, early in the 20th century

About thirty years separates this photograph from the one above.

Above, the sale of agricultural implements, 1910, and below Romford market in the early 1950s. The scene has changed dramatically since the earlier photograph was taken.

.......TO COCKNEY

In the process which heralded the decline of the annual livestock fairs, the itinerant traders who had operated on their fringes and who were beginning to explore the potential of the livestock markets, discovered a guaranteed reservoir of farmers whose wives might be enticed to join them. There was, too, the custom from housewives coming to the market to purchase poultry and dairy produce. Romford market, in its prime position at crossroads on the London Road, promised rich pickings indeed.

This new breed of merchant was akin to the fairground showman with whom he had earlier been forced to compete, barking his wares over the tumult of the holiday crowds and, later, the fairground organ and machinery. He and his fellows entertained the people in Romford market with lively patter and an assortment of gimmicks in order to secure sales, setting up their pitches wherever space became available.

They brought with them a language which derived from an age-old fairground lingo - a medley of words and phrases from the tradionally Nomadic: the language of the Romany, the Back Slang of the Irish tinker, the Yiddish of the Slavonic Jew and the Parlyaree, or Parlare, of those descended from Italian circus folk. Advantageously positioned to colonize Romford market was the Cockney trader who, already steeped in this mongrel jargon and firmly entrenched in the street markets of the East End of London, contributed his own individual brand of colloquialism - Rhyming Slang. An oral tradition which was constantly shifting and changing, exact derivations of this hybrid language, much of which is still in current use in Romford market, have frequently been lost in the mists of time, adulterated through the years by variations in dialect and accent.

The Toby Man
Familiar to all traders on the market, this nickname is given to the Market Superintendent who is responsible for the day-to-day management of the market and collecting rent, or toby money, for the stalls. He was also known, variously, as the toby mush (from moosh, the Romany for man), the toby gorger (gorger being an 18th century word to describe a gentleman) and the tober'omey (from homo, meaning man). The term derives from the early grafters' name for the fairground, and later the market, where they plied their trade - the Tober. Tober is Romany for road, its meaning extended to describe a stopping place on the highway where pots, good luck charms and clothes pegs could be sold. "We had to be on the road early to secure our Toby," recalls one of gypsy ancestry when he was a child in 1910.

Tober, or tobar, was used similarly by Irish tinkers from a very different source - a cryptic language called Shelta which is a type of back slang comprised chiefly of Gaelic words disguised by changes of initial or transposition of letters. Thus, their word appears to be a deliberate perversion of bothar, the Irish for road.

The Kipper Season
In the parlance of present-day market stallholders, this is the period from Christmas to Easter when trade is slack, "the customers are kipping," i.e. sleeping. Another interpretation is that, after the expense of Christmas, people can only afford to buy kippers, once the cheapest of food. During this time, traders are foced to "knock out" their wares at a minimum price just as the shops have their sales. In winter, the old fairground traders abandoned their pitches to go "on the knocker". If the customers wouldn't venture out-of-doors, then the knocker worker would go to them. In Rhyming Slang he was known as the "mozzle and brocha" which was Yiddish for a door-to-door salesman.

The Mock Auction
From the mid-19th century, auctions were introduced to combat the very real problem of individuals by-passing the livestock market to indulge in private deals, the process of bidding guaranteeing a more lucrative, competitive price. So, in the same way that in the past itinerant traders had adopted similar methods to fairground showmen, they now mimicked the style of the auctioneer. Gradually, however, the term "mock auction" came to be associated with a criminal element amongst market traders.

A Glossary of more Market Slang

Parny	Rain. In any outdoor market, where trade is so dependent on the weather, rain is guaranteed to be a prime topic of speculation. The word derives from the Romany for water which, itself, hails from the Hindustani for rain, "pani", serving as a reminder that the Romanies were descended from ancient India.
Parky	Cold, possibly from the conditions existing in an out door space like a public park.
Grafter	Today more frequently used to describe a hard worker, it was originally a term applied to anyone trading at a fair or market.
Spieler	A good, persuasive salesman
Edge	The crowd attracted to a grafter's pitch by the power of hispersuasive spiel, edging nearer all the time.
To come to the bat	After the spiel, the price must be mentioned. It took those selling useful household items like crockery and linen an average of ten minutes "to come to the bat". A quack doctor might take as long as an hour to convince the public of the efficacy of his products.
Hasn't cracked it	Hasn't yet made the first sale of the day.

16

An old style market pitcher beneath a canopy very reminiscent of the fairground, 1907.
Next to Stone's is the old Windmill and Bells inn.

To break the ice
> To make the first sale of the day. An unsuccessful grafter, for example, would too often "come to his bat without breaking".

Gee or rick
> A grafter's accomplice planted in the crowd to set the ball rolling.

Punter
> A rather derogatory term for the customer probably deriving from the word "punt" for a large tankard or mug of beer. The word "punter" was originally applied to someone who knew little about horse racing, betting on horses. In the eyes of the experts, "a big mug".

Pitcher
> A grafter who advertised his wares loudly, often in the style of the auctioneer, although he would bring his prices down while the auctioneer would steer his upwards. A mounted pitcher stood above the crowd. (Not to be confused with a mock auctioneer whose designs were to obtain money dishonestly).

Fly pitcher	Unauthorised person trading illegally
Cheapjack	Not, as commonly believed, one who sells cheap goods but a fly pitcher, a market rogue. Jack derives from the knave in a suit of cards and knave is an old word meaning a rogue. Cheap comes from the old English "chepe" for market.
Gezumph	Yiddish for "to swindle", it is a word now more commonly part of estate agents' jargon.
Lobb	The till. The word was used at least 200 years ago for any kind of box-like container including a till and snuff box.
Joint or gaff	The stall
Flash	An attractive display of goods
Swag	A grafter's stock of cheap commodities especially manufactured for sale in the market.
Plunder	Small items virtually given away in order "to draw an edge".
Kite	A cheque. To fly a kite you have to "raise the wind", wind being a nautical term for money; as necessary to life as wind is to a sailing ship.
The R.O.	An abbreviation for the Run-Out which involves "drawing an edge" in order to conduct a mock auction, usually for nefarious purposes.
Bunce	Money, especially profit
A Buster	A successful day or season
Shice	Yiddish for an unprofitable undertaking. A wash-out.
Cream	Good or best stock
Dealo	Old stock of little use, from the term "a deal suit" - a euphemism for a coffin for the poor. Deal was originally a dimensional term to describe a long, narrow length of wood. It later came to be associated with the cheaper pine woods.
Snodder or Schnorrer	A Yiddish word describing someone who dislikes spending
Lurker	This can either be applied to a potential customer hanging around a stall or a stallholder waiting around for trade.
Knock out	To sell at any price. In the 18th century a person was known as a "knock out" if he combined with another to beat an auctioneer down to a nominal price.

Donah	Woman, from the Italian "donna". A Parlyaree term (Italian: pagliare - to speak). The King's donah was the wife of the Pearly King of the London costermongers.
Mash	A thick mixture of condensed milk and sugar once suppliedin a cardboard cone to the market trader for his cup of tea.
Pot herbs	Vegetables like turnip and swede, used in stews, for which there is little demand nowadays.

Some Slang Terms for The Pound Sterling

Bar, nicker, phunt	One pound
Bottle	Two pounds. Rhyming slang: bottle of spruce (a type of beer) which rhymes with deuce (a two at dice or cards). Originally the term referred to the lesser sum of 2d.
Carpet	Three pounds. Originally applied to a term, or prison sentence, of three months.
Rouf	Four pounds. Back Slang.
Jacks, flim	Five pounds. "Flim" is an abbreviation for flimsy - a slang term applied to bank notes, presumably denoting the quality of the paper on which they were once printed.
Exis	Six pounds. Back Slang.
Nevis, neves	Seven pounds. Back Slang.
Cockle	Ten pounds. This is a good example of how words can become bastardized. Cock and hen, which is Rhyming Slang for ten, became cockernen, which was then abbreviated to cockle.

Market pitchers in the first decade of the 20th century. Owing to its German associations, The Bluchers Head in the background was

EVER BEEN HAD?

It could be very useful for those market traders out to "fleece" the public to indulge in a form of communication universally known to its initiates and seldom comprehensible to anyone else. In fact, some of the words in most common use hinted at exploitation and deceit: the punter, with its mocking overtones, describing the customer; and the grafter's stock - plunder and swag - with their implications of goods illegally obtained.

Tales still circulating round Romford, perhaps embroidered a little over the years, detail sharp practices which could be traced to the market: horses invalided out of the army with bullet holes disguised by boot polish; daffodil heads fixed to their stalks with elastic bands; cauliflowers "mended" by replacing a rotten floret with a clean one painstakingly jig-sawed in; drooping chrysanthemum centres substituted with healthy ones; and the chicken man, stationed outside the old King's Head, who spruced up slightly off chickens by plucking and powdering them, stuffing them with strong herbs and displaying them against an attractive green background of lettuce and cabbage leaves. "His customers came back for more time and again."

Many of the refugees from the annual fairs who were working Romford market during the first half of the 20th century were skilled confidence tricksters, relying for their livelihood on a knowledge of human nature. Their stock-in-trade was the persuasive spiel; their customers, the greedy and the gullible.

The Windbag Worker
Very much the progeny of the fairground, this trader managed to convince the public that the sealed brown envelopes he was selling contained items of some value. He gained his name because most of them contained nothing but air.

The Run-Out Boys
In Romford market, Flash Harry from Aldgate worked "the Run-Out" from the back of his car. His accomplices threw quantities of cheap articles such as notebooks and pencils at passers-by in order to draw a crowd. This was known as "plundering" and, as anticipated, he soon collected a number of people always eager to get something for nothing.

He would next dangle the tempting bait, "the flash", to entice his audience futher, ensuring that it was one of his stooges who caught the real bargains - the silver-plated cigarette case or rolled gold cufflinks - while the crowd gradually grew in confidence. Then a mock auction would begin, with Harry encouraging people to bid for a modestly priced article. Having persuaded half-a-dozen members of the crowd to part with a shilling for a small item such as a butter dish, he would range their purchases in boxes before him and put the money on top of each. These were his "nailers". He had the punters' money but hadn't yet given them anything; he had nailed them down. The rest of the crowd might drift away in search of further diversion, but those who had paid up wouldn't walk away without either their money or goods and he could hold them for as long as he liked.

He would exhort them to buy more expensive items, a watch, perhaps, or a cigarette lighter, making the bargain seem even more attractive, "You were sporting enough to bid me a pound for this watch and I'm going to show everyone what I do with good sports. Here's a solid synthetic gold chain to go with the watch and a pair of gent's cufflinks." In addition to these articles there was, of course, the butter dish. He would then place the customer's pound note on top of the pile, a stratagem known as the M.O.T. or "money on the top", before launching himself into the final dishonest stage of the transaction. "Will you give me two pounds for the lot?" and, at the customer's hesitation, "There's a pound here isn't there that you've paid me for the watch? Bid me two pounds and take the lot. Here, I'll tell you what I'll do as you've been such a good sport. Here's the shilling on top as well. Bid me two pounds and you'll get more than half of what you bid back right away in cash." An irresistible offer and few realised that they were buying back their own guinea (£1.05).

The Fly Pitcher
Not an uncommon sight in Romford today with his easily portable goods, but generally stationed in the open air Liberty shopping centre, or tucked away in odd corners elsewhere, the fly pitcher has always been guaranteed a good living. He has the advantage of being able to follow the crowd and any fines accumulated during the course of the week are regarded as an alternative to the payment of rent.

In earlier years, when policing of the market was not so stringent, the fly pitcher was able to work hard for a few hours and then forget about graft for a time. Even when the weather was bad, he only required a couple of good pitches to make his visit to Romford worthwhile and, better still, if he could stash his gear into a suitcase, he could start work at a moment's notice. The seller of lucky charms could make extravagant promises about their efficaciousness with confidence, telling his customers that if the charms failed to work within ten days they were to return them and he would refund their money two-fold. Where exactly they were to return them to he did not say!

The Quack Doctor
Authority took a dim view of those who avoided paying tolls or worked downright dishonest dodges, like the Run-Out, but adopted a good-humoured tolerance to the purveyors of patent medicines.

In Romford market, this territory was monopolized by the Strong brothers and their father. They were very much the type of perfomers who had frequented the fairs and showgrounds of England. A colourful trio selling all sorts of medicines and elixirs of life, the boys, dressed in traditional strong man outfits, flexed their muscles, pulled chest expanders and lifted dumbells while their father sold home-brewed bottles of "pick-me-up". "It'll make you eat well, sleep well and drink well," (the last statement meeting with an enthusiastic reception from the male spectators). "It'll make you spring out of bed in the morning like a two year-old and sleep at night like an innocent child." The gees planted in the crowd energetically flourished arms miraculously cured from aches and pains as a testament to the Strong's Phosforine lotion, a sovereign remedy for rheumatism.

THE WEDNESDAY CATTLE MARKET REMEMBERED

Memories of the cattle market are dominated by the stench of dung, straw sodden with animal waste, warm milk and the musky odour of shuffling animals, jostling together restively in cramped pens, all overlaid by the pungent, yeasty aroma emanating from the neighbouring brewery. Competing for attention was the noise: of shouting stockmen, fast-talking auctioneers, bleating sheep, cantankerous bulls and, rising above everything, the indignant squealing of pigs as they were manhandled from trucks by their tails and floppy ears. In later years, instead of slapping sold labels on the rumps of livestock, or marking their hides with a red substance, the animals' ears were punched to accommodate buyers' tags (and if the machine was not immediately to hand, then a farmer's teeth would suffice). "My strong memory of the market was the noise of the animals; they always seemed so nervous and frightened. When we had to send our pigs to market, I always kept away." Not yet severed from their rural roots, people on the whole tended to react

Big crowds flocked to watch the horse and cattle auctions in the market before the 1939-45 war. Here, a small Shetland pony is coming under the hammer.

A period of about 70 years separates these two views. Church House, formerly The Cock and Bell, stands to the right of the church.

less sensitively to animal maltreatment but even they could relish the justice meted out by a terrified boar to a lorry driver's mate during unloading. "He was butted headlong down the messy tailboard of the lorry while trying to get the last few stubborn pigs out of the back of the lorry by kicking their heads. He lay sprawled face down in slippery excrement while onlookers gave the pig a hearty cheer and round of applause."

A visit to Romford market on a Wednesday was an eagerly anticipated event, particularly when money was scarce to fund other forms of entertainment. Before the Second World War there were at least fifty pens for sheep, ten for calves and over eighty for pigs, quite apart from the rows of cattle hitched to the iron railings running along the edge of the market plain. The local bus operator, Edward Hillman, ran weekly excursions to the market from Bow at 2/0d return while for those travelling by train from beyond Manor Park it was "a lovely day out. Lots of fields which made it a change from the East End of London." A view of the surrounding countryside could be enjoyed from the top of the market place, too, for the closest farm was only a stone's throw away: Lodge Farm, where Lodge Park is now situated, opposite Raphael Park.

The railway also facilitated the transport of livestock although animals continued to arrive at the market on hoof, "I can remember my grandfather telling me of how, in 1912, he travelled from Ockenden to Kent via the Tilbury ferry to herd sheep from the Romney Marsh to Romford market." Cattle from outlying farms at Chadwell Heath, Collier Row, Noak Hill and Harold Wood were sometimes accompanied by children little more than ten years old. At the railway station Drover Smith, a well-known character, was in charge of rounding up animals which had escaped from the marshalling yard. Here drovers would tout for trade to drive the livestock along South Street to the market place. In their hat bands they would place something to identify their calling; a piece of wool, for instance, to indicate a sheep herder. Those who worked with animals were "a breed unto themselves and were very skilled at handling them." One farrier was so adept at shoeing horses that they could always be identified if "rustlers" had raided local farms. By the 1920s, smaller animals were being packed into rickety trucks with wooden slats along the sides, large tailboards and roofs consisting of rope net.

Organized horse sales had virtually dried up by the end of the 1940s. Mechanized forms of farming made the horse-pulled plough redundant while lorries threatened cart and wagon. Heavy horses began to disappear from town and country and, in subsequent years, thousands were slaughtered. Nevertheless, there remained a demand for the prematurely superannuated horses which lumbered into Romford market from the Ilford Corporation when it finally abandoned its dust carts in the mid-1950s in favour of more sophisticated vehicles. The small farmer still had a use for a strong draught horse and, after all, a good mare could reproduce which was more than could be said for "one of those expensive, new-fangled tractors."

From the early years of the 20th century, all animals were in place in the market by 8.00 a.m, those which had arrived the previous evening being brought from their grazing at Swan Meadow, in the vicinity of the present site of the Town Hall, or from St.Edward's churchyard. Prospective buyers would then view them in time for the auctions at 10.30 a.m. "The cattle were judged by a practised eye and the feel of fat and bone alone," but later a huge weighbridge was introduced to help gauge the price of animals. At 11.00 a.m., after their full milk bags had been inspected, the cows were milked, the dregs from their udders running down in rivulets between the granite cobblestones. "My first encounter with Romford market was in 1935 when my parents moved to the town from the London area. To me it was countryside after a life in the city. The crowds of people all mixed together as one happy family." It was a different tempo of life before the war. Farmers exchanged gossip in the market place while supping a glass of beer, their ponies and traps, in earlier times, left casually in the middle of the market plain. Or they would retire to one of the pubs, always open all day on Wednesdays, to haggle in more comfortable surroundings. In the days before motorised transport, it was not unknown for those somewhat the worse for wear to nod off on the way back from market, their faithful horses unerringly finding the way back home unaided.

A variety of smaller animals were available for rearing or eating. Rabbits had their backs broken and were flung into large baskets. They were highly regarded as an economical meal before myxamotosis was introduced artificially in 1953 to reduce a population which had run out of control during the war. "Lovely red hens" were crammed into wooden crates piled high behind the stall holder. Held aloft for viewing, they could be bought alive or dead, their necks wrung on the spot - very different from today's oven-ready birds: naked, disembowelled, decapitated and quite unrecognizable. Crowds converged around Mr. Bromley's day-old chicks, "pale yellow puff balls" at 1d each (ducklings cost 4d) and Mr. Douglas's plucking competitions. "I can remember clearly to this day the racket of hundreds of squawking hens and, as I travelled home, the cheeping of chickens in boxes on the bus."

Tales of bulls escaping and charging into the proverbial china shop, or stampeding through the Shopping Hall, have become part of Romford's urban mythology, but there can be no doubt that loose cattle were a very real hazard. Bulky, disorientated, hoofs slipping precariously on the cobblestones, they must have presented an alarming sight as they broke away from their keepers. "It was bedlam at times with more and more traffic passing through the market and animals breaking out of their pens." By all accounts, pigs could be an even greater menace. Vicious and bad-tempered, "rusty" in the old Essex dialect, they would fight each other, drawing blood, and, squirming loose at the first opportunity, would charge at full speed. Cows might topple stalls over but pigs, with children in hot pursuit, were harder to avoid and a broken leg could be the penalty paid by the innocent bystander.

The Sheep sales.

The auctioneer trod a catwalk of planks balanced between the pig pens. From a front page feature on Romford Market in the Daily Mirror, 1929.

The animals were as accessible to the general public as those involved in the buying and selling of livestock, with scant regard paid to public health and safety. Embodying the countryman's familiar ease with animals, both adults and children could lean over and stroke them in their pens, mingle with them in the market place or walk down the passageway or a walk down the passageway, on the market's north side, past the market abottoir, Harrison and Barber, without giving cattle pole-axed on the spot so much as a backward glance. A mother taking her small son to market as late as the 1950s recalls him stroking the small calves whose heads protruded from the sacks in which they were trussed up ready for transportation.

On the fringes of the cattle market, and on the side opposite the church where a variety of other stalls operated, farmers sold eggs nestling amongst the straw in large baskets, churns of milk, large cheeses covered with muslin cloths and great slabs of butter. "Butter wasn't sold in packets; it was cut, patted into brick shapes, weighed and wrapped." The sale of fresh butter, stamped with a distinctive design, was one of the perks of the farmer's wife who would also bring baskets of home-grown vegetables to sell, a trade which would all too soon be monopolized, ironically enough, by city dwellers - the barrow boys of the East End who had ventured no closer to orchard or vegetable patch than Covent Garden.

The top, eastern end of the market.

ne Show of Cattle, Romford Market.   118   Pub. by H.W. Hol 60 South St. Rom

Below, cattle being unloaded from a lorry in the late 1940s.

Cattle Market, Romford

The market place in the 1950s. The large weighbridge can be glimpsed on the left.

A Cossack horse troop, 1929, in front of Hollowell's, the horse dealer. The lady standing on the right is Mrs. K.Fowler, one of Mr. Hollowell's seven daughters.

A MARKET "WHO WAS WHO"

Nellie Sims, B.E.M. We have a large plan of the market spread in front of us, dated 1932. Nellie rattles off the names of the stallholders. What a phenomenal memory she has! Perhaps it is rich compensation for the formal education of which she was deprived when seriously ill as a child. So many names are prefixed by "old": old Brownie or old Mr. Chapman, for instance, and yet Nellie, herself, has turned eighty. She is recalling a time when she was just fifteen, a little flower girl working on a stall for the man who was later to become her husband.

A vivid youthful memory particularly stirs her. It was when a troop of Cossacks rode into the market in 1929 to entertain the crowds with their tricks on horseback. One of them especially took her fancy. "Oo, he was 'andsome," she declares with that lovely smile she has, and the years fall away from her.

Nellie and her husband, Harry, longed for their own shop, a dream which came true when the Quadrant Arcade was built in 1935. From their small flower shop was to evolve a charitable enterprise beyond compare, either before or since, in Romford.

Charlie Fancourt Unlike Nellie, this well-known market fishmonger, and one-time meat trader, was to do things in reverse order. He initially rented a shop in the Romford Shopping Hall, paying seventeen shillings a week rent, until lured into the market by the cheaper rate of five shillings. Always the canny businessman, his first instruction to his wife when she was left in charge of the stall during the war was to remember to take the till with her when the air raid warnings sounded. Her reply was unprintable! Charlie was one of a new breed of traders who, once

equipped with motorised transport, left the family business in order to work the markets of south-east England. A neighbouring grocery van in Horsham market, Sussex, belonged to Jack Cohen, the future founder of the Tesco supermarket chain. Charlie joined his father in his Stepney fishmonger's shop as soon as he left school in 1924 and was soon travelling round the markets in a second-hand T-Type Ford van. In the 1930s he based himself in Romford market where his family's fish stall continues to flourish.

Lou Barrett   Known only as Lou, this market character was a particular favourite. Working from his pitch outside the Laurie Hall with his brother, Sam, he sold everything from sugar to bed sheets.   He dealt with awkward urchins in his audience by giving them sweets to clear off, a ploy which back-fired on him as the number of small boys grew in order to partake of this largesse. He also sold war-damaged stock which was not rationed and could be bought without coupons. Lou began his life in Romford market when he took over the Martins' pitch where women's and children's clothes were sold, outside the King's Head. He died in 1995 aged 93.

Bob Sherry   What an enormous selection of old tomes on a variety of subjects were ranged on the shelves of Bob's antiquarian bookstall.   It was with considerable reluctance that, in more recent years, he was forced to concentrate on modern paperbacks to cater for changing tastes. His stall was to be found near the church, close to the old herbal shop owned by his father-in-law, George McClure.   Bob wore a tiny silver caterpillar badge beneath the lapel of his jacket; the insignia of the Caterpillar Club, an exclusive association whose members were those men of the R.A.F. who had successfully baled out of their planes during the Second World War.

Ki-Ki, The Tool King ("ki" pronounced as in "eye").   The real name of this tiny, eccentric trader who sold small tools from his stall close to the church is not known. The young Nellie, watching his antics from her flower stall on the opposite side of the market plain, recalled him dancing like someone demented outside the church whenever a wedding took place, clashing two bricklayer's trowels together as if they were cymbals. He also enjoyed accompanying the Salvation Army band as they passed through the market on the way to their Citadel in London Road. Perhaps his noisy, wild antics inspired his nickname which may have derived from the Romany name for a wild man or wild beast show in the fairgrounds - a Kie Show.

The Gradinsky Brothers sold bananas from an open lorry, cutting hands from huge stalks and throwing the loose ones to the crowd as tasters. Dingle, a present-day trader, worked for them in their North Street shop. **Clarkie, The Banana Man**, was renowned for his generosity. Often, if he spotted a young mum struggling to buy her children a treat, he would give her a big wink and a couple of hands of the fruit.   **The Kent Family** also sold the fruit from the back of a lorry, their pet monkey guaranteed to attract a crowd. Bananas are still considered to be the most popular fruit by today's stallholders and were more so after the war when people had been deprived of them for so long.

Whether **Gertie From Lancashire** actually hailed from that county is a moot point but Lancashire cotton was renowned as the best in the world and everyone went to Gertie's for their curtains.   Like Nellie Sims, she gravitated to a shop which remains, to this day, in Romford.

Ben from Bow, the Chocolate King. "Uncle" Ben Warsham "auctioned" cut-price confectionery, occasionally giving away tasters to the crowd. **Leggett and Baldwin** sold boiled sweets like humbugs and bullseyes which were manufactured in their factory. Archer "Archie" Leggett became Lieutenant of the county and went on to own the Romford Greyhound Stadium which was later sold to Coral's. Cheetah racing was one of the many activities he introduced and it was at Romford Stadium where the cheetah was proved to be the fastest animal on land, a fact frequently recorded in boys' comics of the time, such as "The Eagle". Archer Leggett married one of the seven daughters of Mr. Hollowell who owned the large horse dealer's premises fronting the market place, where C & A now stands.

Len Chase worked on Tyler's egg stall. He was killed in the Second World War at the age of 19, one of many hundreds trapped on the beaches at Dunkirk. He had been married for just one week.

Captain Dyer, seen supping a pint below, was the publican at the King's Head. The dances held in the New King's Hall at the rear of the building were amongst the biggest social events in the town. A long-serving councillor, he became Mayor of the Borough after the war. Local drinkers had him to thank for an extension of the licensing hours in Romford.

Snowy White. You cannot live and trade in an area like Romford market without meeting some "screwball" characters. Snowy was one of these: a great market personality with his irrepressible good humour and fund of practical jokes. Despite this, he was well-liked and respected.

Joe Peacock, not to be confused with **Percy Peacock** who organized pens for sheep and cattle, was a really original character who slept in a wooden shed behind the Romford Shopping Hall. He relied on odd jobs for a living, sometimes acting as a drover or boiling beetroot in an old laundry copper. He is remembered for his contagious laughter and his little white dog, Nutty. Nutty was well-acquainted with all his master's favourite haunts and would scuttle around pubs, betting shops and clubs looking for him.

Billy P. Before gambling on horse racing outside the racecourse was legalized and betting shops were introduced, people had to rely on bookies' runners for a "flutter" or more serious wager. One such was Billy P. who sold newspapers outside Lloyd's Bank, on the corner of the market place. His father, **Old Billy P.**, sold shellfish outside the King's Head for years before anyone else.

Not strictly qualified to line up with the market personages, Miss Bailey, a teacher at St.Edward's infant school near Nursery Walk, will neverthelss be fondly remembered by many of them. She is seen here at her retirement presentation in the 1950s with the Headmaster of the school and the Reverend Wright.

Bill Currie. A fabulous market character, Bill's family still have stalls in the market. He used to drive market traders to various speciality markets in a big van. Even during the Blitz, no amount of dust and dirt would deter him from being smartly turned out in bowler hat, natty suit and immaculately clean shoes. When his own home in North Street was hit by a bomb, he was seen cleaning his shoes amongst the debris

Clockwork was the nickname for a policeman on point duty at the cross roads close to the market entrance whose almost mechanical, regimented movements always attracted a fair-sized crowd. Their laughter was all taken in good part and his last act at the end of his stint was to remove his white gloves and bow to the audience before handing over to his relief.

Ernie Bromley was born in the first decade of the 20th century. He sold poultry, eggs and day-old chicks. His stall was a grand sight at Christmas with a special display of chickens, turkeys and festive fare. He would also sell unwanted puppies and kittens, the proceeds from which went to help old-aged pensioners. He would buy groceries and deliver them to the homes of the elderly.

Billy, The Boxer was a much loved, very vulnerable character who had been a fine figure of a man in his heyday, winning many boxing trophies. Unfortunately, he became "punch drunk" and, in later years, was an inmate of Warley Hospital. Sometimes he would arrive at the market wearing a topcoat over his pyjamas and the hospital had to be notified of his presence there.

Snowball was a well-known tramp who used to earn the odd shilling by helping stallholders pack away and clear up their rubbish. **Peter, The Tramp** was another familiar figure. His real name was Peter Blundell and his home was beneath the Hall Lane flyover on the Southend Arterial Road. Formerly a seaman in the Merchant Navy, he painted nautical subjects on long strips of cardboard which he folded before loading them onto a small pram. They were displayed on the old cattle railings at the top end of the market place. In 1973 Peter was made an honorary member of the Romford Chamber of Commerce.

Nutty Woods. In the days when most people couldn't afford to run a van for their businesses, Nutty thrived with his barrows, trundling clothes, foodstuffs and farm produce from the sidings at Romford Station to the market. He was the town's champion skittle and darts player.

Jack, The Shoe Man "auctioned" footwear at the top end of the market, helping those not so well-off, or mothers with several children, to obtain shoes during the war. He was yet another example of those generous market folk who, although not particularly well-off themselves, were always prepared to assist those who had even less.

The enterprising **Robbie** rented an island stall on the church side of the market where he sold toys. When the hula hoop craze was launched from America on the nation, he kept up with demand by purchasing enormous amounts of coloured plastic hose and recruiting his entire family to cut it up and link it into circles.

A good-humoured, irreverent character, **Amy Foster** always wore a cook's tall hat when serving on her cake stall which she ran from1931. One Saturday she draped some net curtain from Zola's stall over her white overall, grabbed up some flowers and walked up to the church "for a laugh" before the bride arrived. **Old Tom** sold antiques outside the King's Head and **Old Jack** sold clothes for drovers. **Mr.Alfred Rich** was remembered as one of the more important local cattle dealers; and a grandmother recalls her mother telling her of one of the town's wealthier inhabitants , **Mr Brock**, bringing the fireworks manufactured at his factory in Harold Wood down to market in November at the end of the 19th century

Some of the old cattle drovers were remembered by Henry Crossley in his book "Grandfather's Romford".   Dubbed   the   "Wednesday cowboys",   they were **"Drummer" Fox**, **"Smug" Anderson**, **"Tich" Thompson**, **"Tupenny" Finch** and **"Sooty" Poulter,** who was in charge of the parade ring. Other sources have added **Drover Smith**, who was in charge at the station marshalling yard, **"Gander" Vale**, **Mr.Ramsey**, in charge of pigs, and **Tom Burrell**, in charge of calves.

Freddie Frost was better known as **Little Freezer** on account of both his name and diminutive stature (he was only four feet tall). Freddie worked all his life, from boy to pensioner, as a messenger running errands all over Romford, sometimes on his delivery bike. When he worked for Arch's, a grocer's in the market place, people would chuckle to see a large basket coming around a street corner with Freddie hidden behind it. That's how small he was.

Whistling Billy, The Penny Whistle Man, was one of many buskers who entertained the crowds of shoppers, playing the most popular tunes of the day in order to earn a living. He was born in the 1850s and was well into his eighties when he played in Romford market before the war. A fat man, always clad in a long coat and bowler hat, he would never play for money on a Sunday. It was his habit on this day to join in with the Salvation Army band on its Sunday evening march through Romford.

George McClure owned the small herbalist shop,The Botanic Dispensers, close to the church. He had gained an enclopaedic knowledge of herbs from working as a gardener on a 50,000 acre estate in Yorkshire. Many mothers who could not afford to take their sick children to the doctor would purchase one of his tried and trusted remedies such as three penn'orth of camphorated and amber oil to rub on their children's chests. He was regarded as a true gentleman, a good lisrener, and a man with healing hands although he charged nothing for his ministrations. **Claude Humphrey** was another highly regarded local shopkeeper before his premature death at the age of 42 early in 1939. For over fifty years he and his father before him ran "the cake shop in the market place" and were awarded numerous gold, silver and bronze medals for their skills.

Even in a photograph of poor quality, Little Freezer is instantly recognizable.

Mr. and Mrs. Albert Riches outside their home at 61, Market Place, close to the Pig and Pound inn. Cattle were hitched to rails in front of their house.

Prince "I Gotta Horse" Monolulu was famed as a tipster, travelling the race courses and markets of the country. He was held up as an example to aspiring grafters of one who had prospered from an eccentric appearance, his colourful garb, consisting of feathered head gear and long robes, resembling that of an African chieftan.

Mr. Leonard Stone and Mr. Henry Hollowell were members of the market "aristocracy" and Nellie,the little flower girl, had to watch her "ps and qs" when addressing them or their families. Mr.Stone, in his store on the south side of the market place, was a strict disciplinarian who was also very humane. He saved many young girls from a life of drudgery in service, paying them a wage of 10/6d a week and providing bed and board above the store. He would inspect his lady shop assistants' hands, front and back, and ensure that their stocking seams were straight prior to opening the store and personally greeting customers at the door. He lived in a fine house house in Main Road, where Royal Jubilee Court is now. His father, Mr. Denny Stone, founded the original premises in 1864, in order to cash in on the growing popularity of the market.

Mr.Hollowell, who operated as a private horse dealer on the north side of the market place, was a man of some means owning several farms (one in Pettits Lane) where he bred cattle and sheep and grazed his horses. He came to Romford from Northamptonshire where his parents owned a public house and hotel. He came to detest the hotel trade, much preferring the company of the horses in the adjoining stable accommodation.

Messrs Frostick were local sweeps based in the market place. Mr.Henry Crossley in "Grandfather's Romford" remembers them canvassing the streets in a pony and trap with the cry "Sweep, sweep!" After the business folded following the death of Mr.Frostick senior, his son became "a well-known character in and around Romford wearing a Stetson hat and a black patch over one eye."

Albert Webber, born 1904, was Romford's own Father Time. He worked on the railways but repaired clocks in his spare time. He kept the famous clock of St.Edward's church in good working order. It had to be rewound every three days.

Miss Mary Clifton. As this section began with a Lady of the Market, it is perhaps appropriate to end with another. Miss Clifton was known to many for her love of horses and her sharp approach to anything hinting of cruelty to animals. A president of the R.S.P.C.A., she would meet the Chief of Police, an Inspector Denny, after doing her market rounds inspecting the cattle and horses. A number of drovers possessed sticks with a small nail on the end to prod the pigs and cattle in the right direction and woe betide anyone found using them. Once it was known that "The Lady" was in the market, the sticks were quickly hidden from sight. Some of the drovers used to mutter an oath or two when Miss Clifton was around; they were convinced that the pigs used to set up a hollering and squealing to attract her attention when they hadn't been touched.

MEMORIES OF THE SATURDAY MARKET

The general commodities market prospered from modest beginnings on the fringes of the cattle market in the early years of the 19th century until, one-hundred years later, it occupied at least a half of the market plain on Wednesdays and most of it on Saturdays, later spilling over into Fridays, too. Saturday was the most profitable of days for, until about thirty years ago, most people received their pay packets at the end of each week. The market offered a tempting variety of goods for them to spend their money on, either unobtainable from shops or cheaper than shop prices, all sold from a motley assortment of wooden trestle stalls, lorries, vans, carts and barrows.

In common with recollections of the Wednesday market, the smell has lingered over the years in people's remembrances: fish, toffee apples, boiled sweets, vegetables and, in earlier days, the smoking of haddock and herring in the fish curing shed behind the King's Head. A variety of aromas, too, emanated from the shops surrounding the market: the leather goods displayed outside Darke and Smith, the saddlers, the coffee grinder in Wallis's grocery shop, the newly-baked bread from Humphrey's. In those days, "you could cycle into the market, leave your machine unattended and return home laden with cheap fruit and vegetables."

The cries of the pitchers echo in the memory: Lou, of course, and "Lofty" Box, sporting a Tommy Cooper style fez, who was frequently affronted by suspicions of flaws in his reasonably priced material, "There's plenty of walls and

With the number of stalls increasing on Wednesdays, it is difficult to judge whether this photograph was taken on a Wednesday or Saturday.

Romford   Market Place. W.

ceilings but there's no bleedin' flaws." Then there was the volatile "handbag man" appealing to the public, "I'm not asking for two pounds, I'm not even asking for thirty shillings; fifteen bob and it's yours," and flinging good-humoured jibes at the departing backs, "You stingy lot! I could make more money flogging pork sausages outside a synagogue." In more recent times, in the tradition of Lou, it has been Ronnie Saint with his cheerful banter selling everything from toys to electrical equipment, "It's the best bargain you'll get today, darlin'."

But in the arena of the pitcher, it was those who dealt in crockery, with their infinite variety of gimmicks, who drew the largest crowds. They would juggle with china, fan plates out in their hands like a pack of cards, stack dishes along an outstretched arm, clash cups together to prove they were unbreakable ("well, everyone's entitled to one mistake, love,") and build up an eighteen-piece tea set in their arms before throwing it up in the air and catching it intact -all performed against a non-stop flow of persuasive patter. "We children all thought he would drop them and would put our hands over our ears waiting for the crash, but it never came."

One husband and wife team attracted an "edge" by "accidentally" dropping a tray of china, whence would ensue a noisy mock argument. A collection of cracked and chipped crockery was kept expressly for that purpose, looking quite perfect from a distance. To buy something seemed small reward for such entertainment.

Demonstrators, known in the trade as "quiet workers" in contrast to their ebullient neighbours, nevertheless attracted crowds to their stalls by a show of their skills: the toffee maker mixing up butter and sugar into a thick mass resembling several pounds of dough to be hung on a hook at the side of his "joint" and pulled out until it looked like a skein of silvery wool; the clockmaker bent over his intricate repairs; the puppet master; the old lady patiently shredding horse radish into jars; the Indian concocting fragrant perfumes and the seller of cream for corns boiling up a somewhat more noxious potion.

And, over the years, wending their way amongst the teeming crowds were the toy sellers with trays slung around their necks; men with cameras to photograph children holding pigs, parrots or monkeys dressed as dolls; gypsies hawking clothes pegs, heather and predictions; tinkers selling pots and pans; and costermongers carrying huge piles of bushel baskets on their heads with gamblers amongst the traders betting on who could carry the biggest load. It was "a fascinating, adventurous, noisy and lively place." The highspot of the year was the carnival as it passed through the market towards Swan Meadow and, later, Raphael Park. On the day, a bell would sound and that was the signal for high spirits to begin with traders leaving their stalls to run alongside the floats and "bobbies" riding with the procession on bicycles to shepherd things along.

Cages containing canaries, budgerigars and wild native birds hung from stalls, fruit and vegetables were arrayed in delectable display and the flowers - in earlier times all cottage grown - were banked up to make a beautiful sight. Stalls were juxtaposed in cheerful variety, "The levels of trading of the neighbouring pickles and sheet music stalls ran exactly parallel. Although so entirely different in character, they both showed similar profits and losses on the same days."

The Bull in the late 1890s

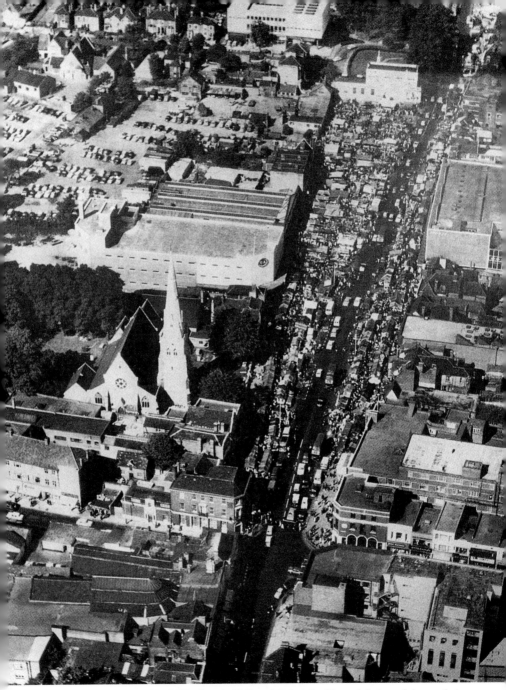

The presence of both The Laurie Hall and C & A in this aerial view of the market indicates that the photograph was taken in the mid 1960s

Shivering, woebegone puppies whimpered and huddled together on the straw in old babies' cots, especially chosen to enable small children to put their hands through the bars and stroke them. Litters of unwanted, blue-eyed puppies and kittens were brought straight to the pet stalls, the mongrel dogs selling at between one pound ten shillings and two pounds ten shillings. Kittens could be bought for a few shillings and no questions asked. "The old paraffin lamps were very bright and hot and kept the tiny creatures warm in the winter." Long before these were used, the stalls were lit by uncovered naptha flares which cast long shadows in the dark winter evenings. The market stayed open until late in those days; 9.00 p.m. on Wednesdays and 7.00 p.m. on Saturdays. The management of the cinema at the top of the market place arranged a late showing of films especially for the market folk.

But while, for many, the market seemed to buzz with the jokes and non-stop laughter of the traders, others found it a frightening, threatening place. Children were at the mercy of clumsy feet and feared losing their mothers. They cringed from the dead rabbits hanging from the meat stalls and from the harsh, bullying tones of the barrow boys. Both young and old disliked "walking on the cobbles and treading on the slippery rubbish on the ground." To one child, Christmas seemed, "a very special time in the market. When I was young, in a way, it almost epitomized that season with its tinsel, light, fruit and carols" while another recalls the frightening crush in the milling December crowds on the pavement and dodging between the traffic on the road which then ran through the market place towards Gallows Corner.

A mother recalled damaging several pairs of shoes from the effort of pushing a pram over the cobblestones; a father, untouched by the magic experienced by his offspring, remembered the "usual, scruffy-looking older men trying to sell you something." A market trader reminisced on the hazards of market life, "It can be very hard, especially in the winter months when snow and ice have to be cleared from the stalls; up at three or four in the morning and rarely home before seven." He recalled a day twenty-five years ago when the market was abandoned in the face of a day-long blizzard, with only three stalls left operating.

The owners of these stalls were, surely, in the true tradition of the old-style itinerant trader who earned his keep by travelling round the fairs and markets of England, arguing against the firm conviction of those grafters with permanent market stalls, that it was no use pitching until the market was in full swing. On the contrary, it was their contention that the secret of making money was to start before the crowds arrived and pitch until dusk.

Above the mother of David O'Brien and her older sister pose for the photographer holding dressed-up monkeys. Below, the grandfather of Graham Wright, on the left of the picture, serves a customer in the 1950s.

A view from the early 1950s.

The Saturday market early to mid 1950s.

The top end of the market in the 1970s. The road through the market was closed to through traffic in 1969. The boarded up site of the Laurie Hall is on the right.

THE PERIMETER

The development of the perimeter almost certainly began with the opening of the market in 1247 and the perimeter premises and businesses would have evolved over the centuries, at first to service and supplement the trading function of the market plain and later to meet the needs of the many visitors to Romford market. Obvious examples of the former would be a requirement for office accommodation for the market administrators together with a place to resolve market disputes and to administer market law, a church for the spiritual well-being of both traders and the local community and then, gradually, the emergence of inns and hostelries for accommodation, refreshment and the stabling of horses as well as a whole range of commercial activities needed to support a thriving market town such as bankers, lawyers, auctioneers, doctors, vets and blacksmiths.

For many years the four landmarks of the market were the Church, the Church House, the Old Court House and the Laurie Hall. **The Church of St.Edward The Confessor and Our Lady** is the market church. Built in 1407, that early church is not the one that we know today for it was demolished in 1847 and rebuilt on the same site in 1850 using some of the materials remaining from the old church together with stone from Nash's Quadrant in London's Regent Street. The major visible change was the addition of a spire to the tower.

One of the earliest photographs taken of Stone's, probably before 1880. (Reproduced by courtesy of Essex Record Office)

Stone's in 1901.

The camera focuses on one of Stone's shop windows c.1900.

The Church House located next to the church and in front of the Wykeham Hall is the oldest surviving building in the market. It dates from the 15th century. Originally built by John Atte Street as a private residence it was purchased by Avery Cornburgh, a courtier of Henry VII, in 1480 and donated to the church to house the parish priest. In the early 17th century it was converted into an inn known as the Cock and Bell and can therefore claim to be the market's first known public house as well as its longest serving one since it was not until 1908 that it reverted once again to the church which then rented it out for a variety of purposes.

The Old Court House stood at the west end of the market place opposite what is now Lloyds Bank and The Lamb. Built in 1826, it was an imposing structure with its mock Grecian pillars which to some extent complemented the Laurie Hall at the other end of the market plain. The Court House served as accommodation for the local police station for many years and contained a number of police cells. In the 1890s the local council used the building for offices and continued to do so well into the 1930s when it was demolished to improve access to the west entrance of the market and to make way for the present Quadrant Arcade. **The Laurie Town Mission Hall** was an equally imposing building standing at the east end of the market approximately where the entrance to the present pedestrian subway is located. It was built c.1850 by John Laurie, a well-known local businessman, and formed part of an imaginative, attractive residential development scheme adjacent to the north-east perimeter of the market known as Laurie Town. Unfortunately the elegant Victorian houses forming the Laurie Square were demolished to make way for the ring road and other central Romford development in the 1960s.

The Perimeter, 1937 Given the difficulties posed by the constantly changing face of the perimeter, we have sought to present a shapshot of one particular time - the year 1937 which was such an important one for Romford with the town achieving the status of a municipal borough by Royal Charter. Much of the market of this period survived into the 1950s and even early 1960s.

The South Side of the Market Place, 1937 Almost opposite the Laurie Hall stood Harry's Cycle Stores whose proprietor, Harry Sibley, was a well-known market figure. This shop, which also sold motorbikes, was flanked by James A.Craig's large furniture stores,"Artistic Home Furnishers" and the Nimbus Ballroom and Restaurant. Close at hand was the old Charity School built in 1728 which then housed the Romford Public Library. The library was opened by the Essex County Council after vociferous petitioning from the Romford Rotary Club and remained in these premises until the library moved across the road to its present palatial three storey building in 1965. Next door was the Romford Market Garage, still owned by the Sharpe family and now situated at the juction of Link Road and St.Edwards Way, and further along the road, in the direction of Gidea Park, was W. Wackett's, the builders' merchant. L.F.Stone, "Draper, Milliner, Costumier and Ladies' Outfitter", became Romford's first department store and, by 1937, towered over the market place.

The point of interest in this photograph, taken prior to 1880, is the colonnaded Court House at the extreme right of the picture. This

With an extended frontage from Nos.60-72, it was taken over by Debenham's shortly before it was due to celebrate its centenary in 1964. Macarthy's, the Chemist, situated close to the Quadrant Arcade, proved to be the longest surviving establishment. It was opened in 1787 and survived Stone's by over twenty years. A drinking fountain was erected in the market place in 1885 as "a testimony of esteem" to C.I.MacCarthy from his fellow townsmen. The Macarthy Mineral Water Company was situated behind the shop.

The public houses on this side of the market were The King's Head Hotel, The Duke of Wellington (formerly known as the Blucher's Head but changed because of anti-German feelings in the First World War), The Swan, and The Bull. The Blacksmith's, J.Cook & Son, operated from the yard at the rear of The Duke of Wellington.

Some notable premises on the south side were, from west to east:
The old Council Offices
Cramphorns Ltd.- Corn and flour merchants (No.24)
Macarthy - Chemist (No.28)
The King's Head Hotel (No.30)
H.Morris - Grocer (No.32)
Forum Ltd.- Confectioner and tobacconist (No.34)
Lewis Cooper - Butcher (No.36)
A.H.Arch - China and glass (No.38) Boot dealer (No.40) Grocer (No.42)
The Duke of Wellington (Nos.44-46)
Benjamin Wallis - Family grocer and provision merchant (No.48)
The Swan Hotel (Nos.50-52)
C.Humphrey - Bakery and tea shop (No.54)
Geo.Copsey & Co.Ltd -
             Romford's oldest house furnisher (and removals) (Nos.56-58)
L.F.Stone & Sons - Department Store (Nos.60-66)
James A.Craig - Draper (No.68)
McChlery & Sons - Butcher (No.70)
R.A.Cornell - Architect (No.72)
The Bull Hotel (No.76)
Stanley C.Barkham - Confectioner and Post Office (No.78)
J.H.Jarvis - Gentlemen's outfitters (Nos.80-82)
Leslie Sheppard - Confectioner (No.84)
Arthur Amery - Boot and shoe dealer (No.86)
Aylett Bros.- Family butcher (No.88)
Joseph Hammond - Builder and undertaker (No.90)
Jessie Bartholomew - Art needlework repository (No.92)
Lilian Bridge - Confectioner (No.94)
James A.Craig, Artistic Home Furnishers (Nos.96-98)
Harry's Cycle Stores (No.106)
The Public Library
Romford Market Garage (No.116)
Gladys Carpenter - Newsagent (No.118)
Alice Burton - Tobacconist (No.122)
Thomas Forster - Chemist (No.124)

The North Side of the Market Place, 1937

Two of the most extensive premises here were occupied by the Romford Shopping Hall, erected in the early 1930s, and the stables fronting the market place, on the site now occupied by C&A, which were owned by Mr.Henry Hollowell. They were accessed through a large archway and his horses would be run up and down the market plain for the benefit of prospective buyers. After his death in 1941 his family struggled to maintain the stables but the age of the horse was over and the land was eventually sold to C&A Modes in the 1960s.

The public houses on this side of the road were situated at either end of the market. The Lamb, which still flourishes today, stood at the western entrance to the market next to S.W.Adams, Romford's leading hardware shop for many years. The Pig and Pound, close to the market's eastern entrance, has not survived but its original signboard can be viewed in the Romford Central Library.

Some premises on the north side of the market were, from west to east:

Lloyd's Bank - Manager, Mr.Rutherford (Nos.1-3)
The Lamb (No.5)
S.W.Adams - General ironmongers (No.7)
Midland Bank - Manager, Lionel Warner (Nos.9-11)
Lloyd and Upton - Solicitors (No.13)
The Canteen Dining Rooms - at one time named The Globe(No.19)
Castle & Son - General printers (No.21)
Darke and Smith - Saddlers (No.23)
Henry Hollowell - Horse dealer and stables (No.25)
I.V.Cummings - Chartered Accountants (No.33)
Quick's Libraries - Bookseller (No.45)
The Laurie Cafe (No.49)
Joseph Wiseman - Linoleum (No.53)
The Pig and Pound - (Nos.55-57)
Frostick & Son - Chimney sweep(No.73)
Livestock auction rooms (No.75)

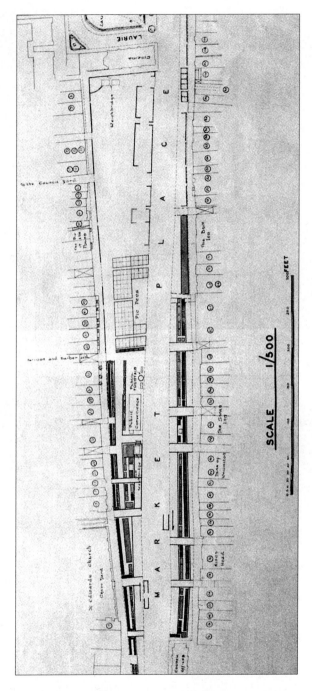

On this plan of the market place, dated 1932, the numbering of premises on the north side begins at No. 13, just before the church, and ends at No. 81, close to the site of the weighbridge (later re-located to a more central area). Part of the un-numbered area between No. 43 and The Pig in the Pound was reserved for the Romford Shopping Hall. On the south side, the numbering begins at No. 16, just after the old Court House (labelled as the Council Offices), and ends at No. 106, opposite the cinema housed in the Laurie Hall.

The old Charity School and Romford Market Garage.
Humphrey's cake shop will be remembered by many Romfordians.

THE MARKET TODAY

For many years Romford's shops and market have existed in relative harmony, the one offering a wider range of products and more comfortable conditions for the customer, the other, with cheaper overheads, supplying a variety of cut-price goods. But the alliance has become an increasingly uneasy one. In order to survive the threat of neighbouring shopping centres, such as Lakeside, and out-of-town superstores, the larger stores have expanded their range of products and priced their goods more competitively, thus having a knock-on effect on market profits.

The market was once at the heart of the town and a focus for celebrations on a grand scale from Queen Victoria's Diamond Jubilee in 1897 to the opening of the Romford Ring Road in 1970. Over twenty-five years later, it is not clear exactly what *is* regarded as the centre of Romford. Since the town's "Golden Mile", South Street, has been pedestrianised and traffic no longer runs through the market, the emphasis has shifted to the Liberty shopping complexes to which all paths seem to lead. The expansion of shopping facilities has proved to be a two-edged sword. Designed to attract more people to the town, it has had the effect of drawing them away from the market. Nevertheless, the market has succeeded in remaining one of Romford's major attractions although it is shrinking in the face of competition. The number of fruit and veg stalls, for example, has dwindled from thirty-five to twenty-five and large areas at the top end of the market are often unoccupied. Shopping habits have changed. People want to park their cars close to the shops and increasing numbers of working wives favour stores which stock a wide variety of goods under one roof. Shopping trolleys do not come amiss, either.

Many of the market stalls, themselves, have increasingly come to resemble shops, providing covered areas in which people can browse and where the stall holders, like so many shop assistants, stand patiently waiting for custom. But the old ways haven't completely died out. Tony Luscombe, pitching in true Lou tradition, "draws an edge" in the notorious "graveyard" area of the market, so-called because, devoid of through traffic, it is a dead end and is not patronised by as many customers. Outside the church, Wickenden Meats continue to prove the efficacy of non-stop patter, as does Steve Bowley, a casual trader from Derbyshire who sells towels.

The market, too, can still boast several colourful characters, if not in the same numbers as yesteryear: Brummy of Southend whose family left the Midlands following the devastationof the war; Mr.Brandon, 85 years of age and still working from time to time on the family fruit and veg stall, who entertained us with some old Cockney costermonger songs; and Ernie Preedy who shared his rich memories of the effect of the war on the market with us. Eels and shellfish could be bought off the ration, tomatoes were a rare luxury and a melon could cost a week's wages on the black market.

Then there are the well-known traders of later generations - Billy Beet who earned his nickname from boiling beetroots after school for his father's stall; and Ray the Lamp who has been stuck with this "monniker" since he was eighteen,

A discerning customer in the 1980s

working for Jim Currie fuelling and lighting the old paraffin lamps which used to illuminate the stalls. Jim's family continue to run a stall on the market as they have done for over a hundred years: fruit and veg before the war, then biscuits and now cosmetics. As "young" Jim told us, "You couldn't have run a cosmetic stall fifty years ago. The only thing you could have sold was Lifebuoy soap." Other established market families continue to flourish: The Fancourts, the Riders, the Ports and the Chapmans.

The market is better regulated nowadays. Strict health regulations have prohibited the sale of live poultry and pets, fly pitchers are soon seen off and gone are the days of the barrow boys who, under the leadership of Billy Stratford, the "barrister barrow boy", fought unsuccessfully throughout the 1970s for their right to pitch in any available space despite blocking public access. They even pushed their heavy barrows all the way to Whitehall to petition the powers that be.

One of the few facets of Romford's history which has not been destroyed by the developers, the market beat off an attempt by an organization called the Romford Imps to close it down in the 1930s because of its down-at-heel appearance and, as recently as 1989, fought off a challenge from the Borough of Redbridge to establish a market in Ilford. The issue went before Parliament which upheld the ancient decree that no other market could be held within one day's drive of sheep and cattle from Romford - a distance judged to be six and two thirds of a mile - as pronounced by King Henry III 750 years ago.